How
disap

Haytham El-Wardany

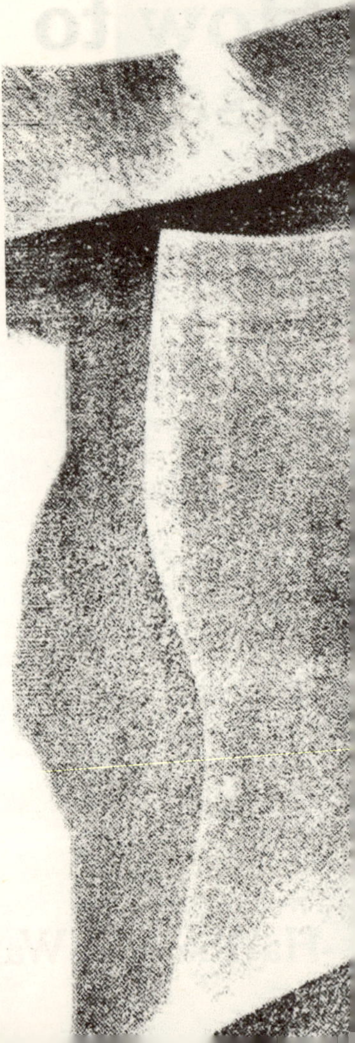

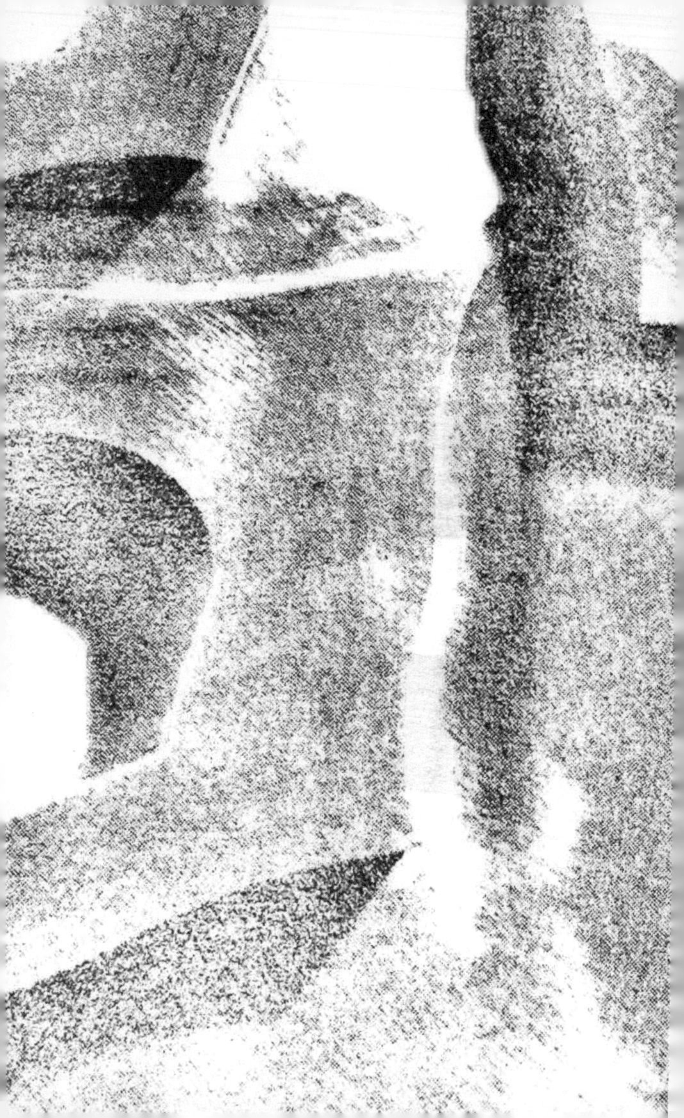

Preliminary Excercises

(Annex) Sounds of the Middle Classes

Preliminary Exercises

HOW TO DISAPPEAR

1. Sit alone in a public space like a café, garden, or public square.

2. Try to shift your focus from the thoughts spinning in your mind to the sounds of the space surrounding you.

3. Consider the sounds that reach your ear, sound by sound, without granting any one sound greater significance than any other.

4. Contemplate the folds and creases of the sounds you now hear. When you hear the voice of a passerby, contemplate its tone and this tone's depth, not only the meaning of its words. When an annoying car drives past, contemplate the harsh sound of its motor and the sonic spectrum of its reverberations. When you hear a distant radio, don't focus merely on the singer's voice or the song's name, but rather contemplate the clarity of its frequency and listen to its static.

5. Prevent these sounds from forming a hierarchy; prevent them from occupying the foreground or retreating to the background. Always remember that you must place all sounds at the same distance from you.

6. You will find that your greatest difficulty is concentrating on the sounds themselves, for the thoughts, impressions, and memories that these sounds conjure up will persistently take over part of your concentration, pushing the real-time sounds to the background. Make sustained efforts to return to the sounds arising in your present moment, for your mission is only to listen to them, not to think about their meanings.

7. As time passes and you steep yourself in what you hear, you will discover an increasing number of sonic details around you. Each of these details will lead you to another; each sound will lead you to a neighboring one. At this point you will find that your inner voice gradually diminishes at the same rate by which you immerse yourself in your sonic environment.

8. When you ultimately succeed in listening to the place in its entirety, you will find that the distance between yourself and the space's sounds has diminished, and that you have become part of the place. You will find that no one around you notices your presence; everyone will pass by without seeing you.

HOW TO REAPPEAR

1. Return home and turn on all the electrical appliances you own. Run the vacuum cleaner at full power, turn the radio and television on at full volume, turn the air conditioning on if you have it, run the washing machine, and, if you have one, set the alarm clock to go off.

2. Sit for half an hour amidst this maddening cacophony.

3. Allow the sound waves to sweep away any thoughts or impressions you may have. Contemplate the impossibility of focusing your attention on any one thought.

4. Half an hour later, turn the electrical appliances off one after the other.

5. Sit in the silence left behind by the aborted noise and try to relax. You will hear a vague drone, the sonic vacuum created by the halted churning of the atmosphere.

6. You will slowly notice that your self is rising to the surface of your consciousness in the form of cohesive lumps of forgotten moments, exactly like

lumps of cheese rising to the surface of curdled milk. Your self will begin to regain its unity that was nearly lost in the storm of external cacophony. The risen moments will float before you in silence. Some are fleeting moments from your past that you recognize; you are unsure of the source of others, but sense that they are part of you.

HOW TO LISTEN TO YOUR INNER VOICE

1. Undertake a number of reading sessions.

2. In the first session, read what you like in the field of history. Let it be Roads and Kingdoms by Ibn Hawqal. Notice how the written words that your eyes fall upon are transformed into sounds that ring directly in your inner ear. Note also how this voice reciting words within you is connected to the degree of your concentration, for the more you concentrate the more clearly you hear this voice, and the less you concentrate due to the clarity of the written words or due to exhaustion, the more this voice retreats.

3. In the second session, read what you like in the field of philosophy. Let it be the *Dialogues of Plato*. While reading, ask yourself whether there is a difference between the voice you hear now and the voice you heard during the first session.

4. If your response is that there is no difference, this means that the voice you heard while reading was not the voice of history or of truth or of one of the authors, but more likely your own voice. Yet is this voice the external voice you speak with, and which you hear when you speak?

5. In the third session, read what you like of poetry. Let it be the work of Salah Abdel-Sabur. Pay attention to the clarity with which the voice now appears. Notice how its echo rings in your ear, and how the verses become embodied thanks to this voice. Now that it has become clear, listen to this voice anew and become acquainted with its characteristics. You will notice that it resembles your external voice but is not an exact copy of it, for the state of your external voice does not affect that of your inner voice. Your inner voice reading words to you does not change, even if you are congested or have a cough or suffer from insomnia. Your inner voice does not necessarily conform to the stage of life you are in, for it is ageless. It is the same voice that you have refined throughout your life.

6. In the fourth session read a novel. Let it be *Crime and Punishment* by Dostoyevsky. Change the rate at which you read. Start by slowing down and halt briefly after each word. While you are reading, listen to the sound of the words within you. Notice how clear the voice sounds. Then increase the speed until your eyes can barely catch the words on the page. Notice how the sound breaks up. Yet you will

notice that in both cases the voice does not change its tone. Slowness has not made it heavy and rapidity has not made it sharp, as we are accustomed to in recorded cassette tapes. This is the second characteristic of this voice, for it is a unique and distilled essence whose nature does not change.

7. Leave the novel aside and recall its story. You'll find that the voice recalling the events and situations in the novel is the same voice you heard while reading, even though it's not using the same words but rather your personal vocabulary and your own ordering of events. Resume reading and note that the voice you hear within you as you read is identical to the voice you hear within you as you think. This means that your inner voice—that closest to you and the voice in which your self declares its presence—bespeaks ideas, emotions, and memories not specific to you but rather to the author. Next contemplate the fact that those thoughts, feelings, and memories contained by the voice of the author but articulated by your inner tongue in turn belong to other people as well. Contemplate the fact that your inner voice, at this moment, is nothing more than the voices of others that have become part of you, for all

these thoughts, emotions, and external words that your body has not experienced have now been transferred within you and blended with your being. This is the third and final characteristic of this voice; your internal voice is nothing more than the sound of the exterior world resounding within you after having acquired your unique tone.

HOW TO FIND MEANING IN DEAD TIME

1. If you sit in your room for hours on end with nothing to do, place an empty cassette tape in the player and press the record button.

2. The player will record the sounds of your room on the cassette tape: passing sounds drafting in through the window and random interior sounds like the opening or closing of a door, the compression of the mattress if you sit on the bed, water passing through pipes located near your room, the telephone ringing if someone calls you, and the room's murmurings of no identifiable source.

3. Listen to the tape you have recorded.

4. You will be struck with boredom the first time you listen to these random sounds devoid of any meaning.

5. Overcome your sense of boredom and listen a second, third, and fourth time.

6. Starting with the fifth time you listen, you will begin discovering meaning in the sounds you hear. You will sense that their ordering is not haphazard, as you had thought, but rather that

a clear logic governs them, as though a musical genius had composed them. The formerly random sounds are now organically inter-joined. As soon as you hear the window hinge moving, for example, it is only logical to immediately hear a car passing by on the street.

7. Listen one more time. Note that what you are hearing is the sound of long, empty hours, and that the new-found meaning that you have gradually grown accustomed to is that very emptiness you had been experiencing, now abstracted from your feelings, and thoughts, and presence. You will discover that emptiness is not in itself an absence of all meaning, but rather your inability to understand new meaning.

HOW TO CHANGE YOUR FREQUENCY

1. Allow yourself the freedom to spontaneously intervene in what you hear around you.

2. Upon hearing a statement that catches your attention, whether at work, home, or on the street, don't hesitate to comment on it, whether negatively or positively, even if it was not directed to you.

3. Note how your tongue and ear have merged to become a single organ that, like all bodily organs, transforms the material that enters it. What enters the ear exits on the tongue after having been made into something else.

4. After some time, stop immediately intervening in the conversations of those around you and instead spend most of your time alone at home. Refrain from meeting people and abstain from speaking as much as possible. Following a sufficient amount of time, you will find yourself sitting alone and articulating speech directed at interlocutors who are not present. You will continue cut-off conversations with them, or suggest better solutions to crises you had together failed to resolve.

5. At this point you may realize that in both cases, the origin of speech is a response to an external call, whether from real or imagined speakers. It is a response based on receiving an incoming wave, and then retransmitting it after slightly altering it.

6. Next return to your accustomed way of speaking. Reflect on what you say when speaking with someone naturally.

7. Note that natural speech is a balance of the two situations described above, for your response in a natural situation is neither spontaneous nor fragmented as in the first case; it is neither contemplative nor poetic as in the second. The state of your normal speech results from a blend of your focus on the present moment and your continued dialogue with thousands of past moments. This blend grants you the opportunity to plan and then respond appropriately; it creates a specific frequency that sets the tempo of your response.

8. Note also that when speaking naturally, your speech is in general a response to what you hear. Yet as your natural speech is a compromise between

these two cases, it not only includes a response to those speaking to you, but also to those not present, those whose words continue ringing in your ears despite their physical absence.

9. Changing your frequency means repositioning the point that represents your natural state on a tuner for which the spontaneity of the present moment forms one extreme and the poeticism of daydreams forms the other. The key to doing this lies in adjusting your distance from non-present interlocutors. The stronger your connection with them, the weaker your frequency, the more tenuous your attention, and the closer your speech to the domain of dreams. The weaker your response to them and the more you focus on the present moment, the stronger your frequency and the more your speech is conjoined to the reality of the present.

HOW TO JOIN A GROUP

1. Select a number of public spaces in which you can sit throughout the day, such as a café or waiting room.

2. Allocate to each space a maximum of one hour.

3. When you enter a space, notice the subtle sound adjustment that takes place as those present notice your entrance. It's an adjustment that may include a lowered sound level or a sudden halt to some conversations. The degree to which the place's sounds adjust depends on the kind of place it is; the more spacious, the less change there will be. If you enter a train station, for example, the adjustment in sound affected by your arrival will hardly be noticeable. If you enter a café where only a few patrons are sitting, however, the change in sound will be substantial.

4. Observe the slight tension circulating the place due to your silent sitting, especially if everyone else had been absorbed in conversation. Observe your unfamiliarity with the place, especially if this is the first time you've sat there.

5. You can now use your silence to measure the cohesiveness of the group surrounding you. If it's a close group in which all the members share a common tie, they will be disturbed by your silence, which may be frightening to them and understood as a departure from the group and a show of superiority. Yet if it's a loosely formed group consisting of randomly scattered individuals, your silence will be overlooked.

6. In either case hold tight to your silence and wait.

7. Following some time, its length depending on the type of group, the sonic environment will return to its previously established nature. As you sit in silence, allow your attention to shift randomly between the conversations you hear. Notice the sonic adjacency of them, and how each conversation taking place is aurally reliant on the conversation beside it, as though it were seeking company or reassurance in it. Contemplate how the conversations taking place remain adjacent to each other without overpowering one another or cutting each other off. Instead, they enter a relationship similar to that of spatial adjacency; they form a sonic neighborhood. The speakers know that their neighbors

are capable of listening to what they're saying and yet this doesn't make them whisper or refrain from private conversations so long as they can hear the continued mumble of other neighboring conversations.

8. Spend a few moments contemplating this sonic neighborhood you are now sitting in. Let yourself soak it in. You will realize that you are no longer separate from it, and that a vague sense of solidarity has crept into you as a result of your compatibility with the group around you.

9. You must distinguish between two types of solidarity depending on the kind of group around you. The solidarity of a cohesive group is felt in its acceptance of your presence on its periphery as your silence is transformed from a black hole swallowing the group's conversations to a gateway through which these conversations can pass. The solidarity of a loosely formed group allows a return to yourself and the widening of your lake of silence as you locate space for it.

10. If you fail to sense solidarity, despair not. Hold on to your silence and wait. This is another

way to connect with a group—connection through compulsion.

11. Whether you sense solidarity or not, get up after an hour and repeat the experience in another place to learn the virtue of moving between groups.

HOW TO BREAK WITH A GROUP

1. Leave your house and walk aimlessly through the crowded streets of the city.

2. Disengage from everything that has taken place in your day, and let your ears pick up everything happening around you.

3. Listen to the particles of sound that fill your ears as you walk: doormen shouting, vendors crying, grocers playing Qur'an, bakers working at their hissing ovens, waiters clattering coffee cups, laborers slaving with pickaxes, soldiers shuffling in heavy boots, public transport drivers rumbling along with their buses, microbus drivers blasting their songs, delivery boys on sputtering motorcycles, the rich roaring along in new jeeps, police wailing with their sirens, merchants partying at cacophonous weddings, youths turning up their latest ringtones, shoppers clamorously bargaining, criminals firing their guns, dogs barking.

4. Observe the multitude of social classes and structures that collide until dissolving into minute particles floating through the subconscious of the city.

5. Try to connect the waves of your own subconscious to those of the city.

6. This will produce a unique motor of sorts.

7. Notice how this motor spins roughly and unevenly.

8. Continue your walk and notice that as the motor spins, the city reaches its limit and begins to rant in delirium. This delirium extends in all directions and comprises all periods of time. With each turn of the motor, one age intertwines with another and your position within it is pulled from one extreme to the next. Note that you are no longer observing this expansive delirium, but rather you are in the very heart of it.

9. You are now a runaway slave. You are now an ordering lord. You are now a lost dog. You are now a winged bird.

10. You will not be able to tell when the motor stopped turning, nor how the layers of this raving delirium coagulated. Yet you will notice after a few moments or minutes or hours that you need to

sit down to catch your breath, and that the particles of sound are now being ordered in the form of sentences, and that the sentences are making their way to your tongue, and that your tongue is asking about the way.

11. When the motor comes to a complete stop, you will have returned to your day that looks onto your life that looks onto the history of the city.

ANNEX

Sounds of the Middle Classes

Inner Peace:
a continuous metallic hum transmitted through air or passing through walls punctuated from time to time by a coughing shudder.

The sealed space is the grail of the middle class and its paradise. There, it dwells and toils and breeds and dies. Wide open spaces are a source of danger, where uncontrollable, indecorous social forces riot and roil. The middle class moves between two sealed spaces, with the street that joins them the Purgatory that must be crossed to reach paradise. Should the need arise for them to walk abroad, they scamper in terror through the street—which has become a battlefield—until they make it to the Inside and are blessed with security and calm. The guardian angel of this paradise is the air conditioner. There is nothing more effective at abstracting a space and resetting it within clear boundaries. It exercises stringent control over entryways and exits on the pretext of preserving inner peace, vigilant for the slightest chink in those dividing lines, which would lead to the pandemonium of the outside infiltrating once more inside. And its purpose is exactly this. Its role is not confined to isolating the inner space by means of controlling the temperature and humidity but goes further, utterly abolishing the outside by separating it off sonically as well as climactically. Only those without can grasp the full meaning of this, for they are the ones who hear the air conditioners' thrum and roar while those within sit mesmerized by the whispered hiss of their machines pumping treated air through their rooms, the outside barely heard at all.

Barter:
a muted storm of footsteps rushing back and forth, swelling gradually then suddenly breaking off with the sound of a violent collision.

The kids, forbidden from playing in the street are tramping out new streets inside their homes: safe streets beneath the eyes of their elders where no harm may befall them, where they might meet no strangers. Between the great lumps of furniture that throng the flat, young feet at play cut narrow pathways that slowly widen with each centimeter won: a push here; a nudge there. But the true essence of the interior roads fashioned by these youngsters is not that they are geographical pathways, but rather sonic zones designed to barter for freedom with noise. The implicit contract is that the adults prevent the children from going into the street, where sounds and voices mingle, and in return the children are allowed to make a racket that is contained by the four walls of their home and which the adults are able to bear. The noise made by the self-absorbed children gets ever louder, yet no one minds: the adults' ears are trained to ignore what they don't wish to hear. Until, that is, the noise exceeds the permitted bounds and constitutes a threat to the order of the home. For instance, when they finally manage to tip the dining room table over or band together to rip down one of the heavy curtains. Then, the contract is broken on the spot and the adults roar out commands, repealing the right to make a din. The game stops, the kids withdraw to a corner, and a wary calm descends.

Out of control:
at 6am each day a woman screams, "Shame on you! You want to drive me mad? Shame on you, you little savages! Shame!"

In that instant, before the day's wheel starts to turn again, her self-control gives way, and her shrieking gathers in volume as she pursues her staggering, stumbling children from room to room, before her voice cracks: "What more do you want from me? Shame on you!" The children's mistakes and blunders mount and her madness grows accordingly. The boy hasn't finished his breakfast egg, the girl's not put her schoolbooks in her bag. "This is too much! Enough!" and she starts to wail. At this early hour her voice, normally unheard, dominates the rest of the household; it bursts out suddenly, a raging torrent sweeping away everything in its path. At last the stunned kids leave for school, the door slams shut behind them and her hour of madness is over. She sits alone, surrounded by the spectres of the terror her screeching left in its wake, until, gradually, the pain dies down—the pain whose source she does not know—and the daily routine slowly begins. Here, in the world of things, are paths she will sketch out and changes she will opt for. She roams this world amidst the roar of appliances: the television talks, the hoover sucks, the washing machine tumbles, the gas stove hisses. Now and then, her shy voice surfaces, calling to the doorman to fetch her groceries, but this time it bears no trace of the morning's ghosts.

Call:

a window opens and voice calls out: "Hey, Abou Sayyid!" The call's repeated, louder each time, until its intended recipient hears. Should this fail, the caller changes the name, "Sayyid! ... Mohammed! ... Ola!" and so on, till one of these names obeys the call.

Squalid social mores dictate that when two classes meet, the higher retains the right to speak and the lower holds its peace. You rarely hear any voice coming from the apartment which houses that family whose precise number is a mystery to everyone—unlike the homes which issue calls, which throb with air conditioners and television blare, which ring to the sound of childish play and shouts. After the call, a member of that family emerges to say, "Yes, ya Basha?" or "Can I help, ya Bey?" Then the command to ascend comes down and he ascends; the order to buy some article or other arrives and off he goes. The call is a summary of relations between two populations who divvy up the street between them. The caller awaits an answer: thus, he grants the callee permission to appear. Not in order to talk with him, no, but to answer a command or demand. The callees in turn may not call out to the callers. When the former have carried out their appointed tasks they go up and politely knock on the door to let the latter know the outcome. Only in those dead hours during the day, when every home is absorbed in its own affairs, can Abou Sayyid be heard bickering with Umm Sayyid in the accent they're careful to hide when speaking with the callers. Only then does Ola fiddle with her father's mobile phone, the strains of a street gig hit floating out. Only then does the laughter of Mohammed and his mother rise up, as she picks lice off him in the sunshine.

Homeless:
at 6pm each day a man shouts, "I've told you a hundred times: no one move anything of mine from its place!"

They all cower where they sit, without responding, while he clumps irritably through the cramped rooms, sweeping everything on the table to one side then pushing it back all disordered, opening and slamming doors, lifting things and laying them down, jerking drawers and emptying them out. How could anything vanish in a tiny place like this? The list of vanished objects grows longer by the day: pens, cassette tapes, socks, small screwdrivers, water bottles, plastic flowerpots, keys for locks that no longer exist, old papers. This time he is looking for a blue lighter. His young daughter thinks to help him: "The one you're looking for doesn't work, but this one does." He looks at her and barks, "A hundred times! A hundred times I've said no one touches my things, whatever they are!" Then he looks at his wife and goes on raging: "Get it into your heads! This is no way to live!" Each time something disappears, something new and unexpected surfaces from the apartment's innards and a whole world of other things opens up: things no one remembers, things tucked away in tins and drawers and shelves. The cares of big city life haunt the air and their house grows ever more cramped. An hour goes by as he circles like a madman amidst this detritus while the rest sit silent. It is no longer the lighter—or any other object—that drives his quest, but rather something else, something bigger, that belongs to him. For an hour he keeps at it, until he's had enough. He dresses and goes out, slamming the door behind him, hard.

Pulse:

the spluttering of a motorcycle's engine cut through the neighbourhood. The engine pops and crackles like a machine gun, coughing out erratic gouts of exhaust. Its echoes bounce from house to house, until the bike pulls up outside one of the buildings and the engine cuts.

Were this a fairytale, the driver would be a genie, the customer the lucky man who'd stumbled on the lamp and the bike-borne goods his wish, granted in an eye-blink. For the goods are no longer carried or fetched, but fly straight to the customer's door. He has but to whisper their name and they are immediately dispatched from where they sit and carried swiftly through the city streets by the driver who arrives with them safe and sound in his hands and rings the bell. And because there are no real genies, wishes, or lucky fellows in this kingdom, and no magic lamps that let their owner turn things into other things, the customer opens his front door, and takes the goods … and pays the bill. During the course of the short transaction between customer and driver a pulse runs through the kingdom. A shiver, rapid and faint, but encompassing vast distances nonetheless. The magic in fairytales is a real magic, which moves and swaps things round. It makes the frog a prince, turns dust to gold. The magic in our world is an imposter. It makes no substitutions, just allows things to encompass vast distances without ever leaving their place. There is the distance between the place of production and the customer's home: a misleading distance in an age in which homeowners are accustomed to choose from products which have been produced in a number of different locations simultaneously; there is the distance travelled by the driver, from his home in some thicket of the urban jungle to the motorcycle mechanic in another, to ensure the engine is up to the task ahead; or the distance the customer travels in his air-conditioned car to work; the distances dividing the city's districts, traversed by people and goods. All these distances are encompassed in a fleeting, magical pulse, without anybody swapping their position … and everything is transformed, just as in our fairytale. The kingdom exchanges its products with itself via those who move and travel, without the travelers exchanging their places. So it is that each time the echoes of a motorcycle's spluttering engine bounce from house to house, the kingdom thrills to a new pulse running though its veins.

Leakage:

the roar of a motor. The motor keeps cutting out, with a thudding tick. If the automatic starter breaks, the motor never cuts out: the roar keeps going until it turns to a hum or growl.

All the apartments in this building have leaks. The pipes snake across the walls, their entry and exit points embellished with large damp spots. The man on the first floor complains that water rises into his apartment from his manifold drain openings, forcing him to block them all except one which he raised up twice as high. The bedroom ceiling of the fellow on the second floor regularly flakes and crumbles because the water pipe of his third floor neighbor is not adequately sealed. Another third floor resident has a mysterious water pipe that seems to come from the roof and emerges through his kitchen wall. He stuffed it with old newspaper but it traps air in winter and brown mildewy drops seep out. The pipe is not connected to anything and no one knows what it is for. He once considered removing it, but his laziness put paid to that idea after he noticed he would have to detach it from its fixing brackets along all his neighbours' windows. Up on the fourth floor, a resident is always being surprised by new sources of water—creeping out from beneath the fridge, a small puddle under the stove—and every time he discovers yet another mains connection which he was previously unaware of, installed by some former tenant when he changed the plumbing. For some reason, the obsolete mains connections in this building can occasionally leak water. Everyone complains that the automatic starter never lasts longer than a month or two. They squabble over the motor and over the cost of repairing things that the water has damaged in their homes. Sometimes, one of them might fail to pay his share of the new starter. The motor's left running day and night only to burn out when the water is cut off. New negotiations get underway, which result in a subscription to repair the motor and buy a new starter, and the cycle begins again. The plumber who comes each time to repair the damage tells them it's a strange building and they nod. He tells them the new starter won't last longer than a month or two unless the leaks stop, and they nod their heads again.

Emptiness:

a guard dog's whine splits the evening hush, punctuated by the distant barking of a pack of strays.

On the edge of this empty patch out of which the city rises and crests, a man stands on his balcony, facing the emptiness, alone. Only the grunts of the guard dog lurking on his balcony can still his terror of the nebulous forces that hover over the darkened void. He finishes feeding the dog and lights a cigarette, confidently leaning out over the wastes with his dog beside him whining ever louder in the direction of the empty ground. The terror vaporizes and the void is filled with a towering sonic edifice. The man pats the dog, "Good boy, Seif," then turns to go inside. But before he can slide the balcony's glass door open the sound of barking, distant and dispersed, reaches his ears. He freezes and Seif breaks from his side, surging to the balcony's low wall, and starts to bark. The man tries to guess how far away the sound is, to imagine the faces of this pack of strays. He sees them trotting along with drooling muzzles, dust on their backs, their legs caked black from dips in stagnant pools. Their drawn faces draw nearer: festering muzzles, pairs of eyes that belong to nameless creatures.

The man holds his position before the door, his back to the empty ground, and through the glass he sees his wife and his two children drowsily watching the TV. He strains his ears to catch the pack's barks through Seif's deafening yelps, and can hear them start to weaken before his dog's superior force. He waits another minute, till he is quite sure that the distant barking has disappeared, then turns to give Seif a final pat. He pulls the glass door and heads into the room.

Panic:
an indistinct hubbub in the distance. A blend of bellowing mob and indecipherable chanting. It persists for a moment then is gone. It is impossible to be certain where it comes from or even to know if it is real or imagined.

When the city was left to look after itself, the revolution could exist nowhere but in story: either in the deepest interior (i.e. the imagination) or in the deepest exterior (i.e. downtown). And so, as it approaches the apartment on its way to the adjoining street, or the next one along, dream blends with reality. Does all this din and clamour signify a real demonstration down below, or is it just a fight between the neighbours? Are those real voices, or has madness turned the backing track of news reports into an echo chamber of chanting in our heads? Whatever its source, the indistinct hubbub provokes panic and clutches at hearts and amid all the confusion difficult questions raise their heads and demand that choices be made. Should you leave your home to see what's going on, if only from simple curiosity? Or should you remain to defend the place in case of attack? What's the significance of what is taking place? What do they mean by "revolution"? Will a Molotov cocktail start a blaze that will engulf the whole building? Should you repark the car so it doesn't get damaged? But when the waves of noise recede, carrying these questions with them, peace of mind does not return. The panic remains; one's fears that the outside world is the ultimate source of danger are confirmed. Everything that comes from out there is beyond all comprehension, impossible to predict, and if a man doesn't keep his wits about him the next wave will be higher still and wash away all he's built. The doors and windows are firmly secured and bolted against the coming blow.

Ecstasy:
bomb clap, rocket whistle, candle pop, gun boom, explosions.

On Eid eve the city suddenly transforms into Marinetti's metropolis of the future. It fuses into a single collective project whose sole concern is breaking the sound barrier. Everyone leaves their homes and comes onto the streets. Corners and alleyways heave with people from every walk of life and type, side by side, men and women, young and old, rich and poor, gents and urchins, turncoats and the true, and every one of them wants no more than to hurl what's in their hand and add another bang to the sea of bangs about them. With every new detonation, however small, a new soul is freed from its straightjacket to melt into the undifferentiated sonic embrace. All the forces that have divided up the city and chopped it into classes, now join in a melting pot of noise and percussive blasts. The Future City spreads out through space like a single raging wave of endless explosions unmixed with melody or rhythm, an ecstatic flood of din and clap and boom, then more, then more again. But on Eid morning the explosions end. The rabble gradually withdraw and the city's forces return, orderly, to work: the steady symphony. Why is it that this war, begun by the Future City, does not persist, grow into a universal war that shakes the foundations of the whole planet? Why does everyone go home again? Maybe because the old city never went away. The exception it allows on Eid eve is the trick by which it proves the rule, the foundation, on which its homes are built.

How to disappear
by Haytham El-Wardany

This publication is the first in the Kayfa ta series. The text was originally authored in Arabic.

Commissioning editors
Maha Maamoun and Ala Younis

Translators
Jennifer Peterson
"Preliminary Exercises"
Robin Moger
"Sounds of the Middle Classes"

Design
Julie Peeters

Printers
53dots, Beirut

Publisher
Kayfa ta
www.kayfa-ta.com

ISBN 978-1-955702-06-5

First edition, Zagreb 2013
Second edition, Hong Kong 2014
Third edition, Beirut 2014
Fourth edition, Cairo/Berlin 2018
Fifth edition, Beirut 2021
Sixth edition, Beirut 2025

Kayfa ta is an independent publishing initiative founded in 2012 by Maha Maamoun and Ala Younis.

كيف تــ
KAYFA TA